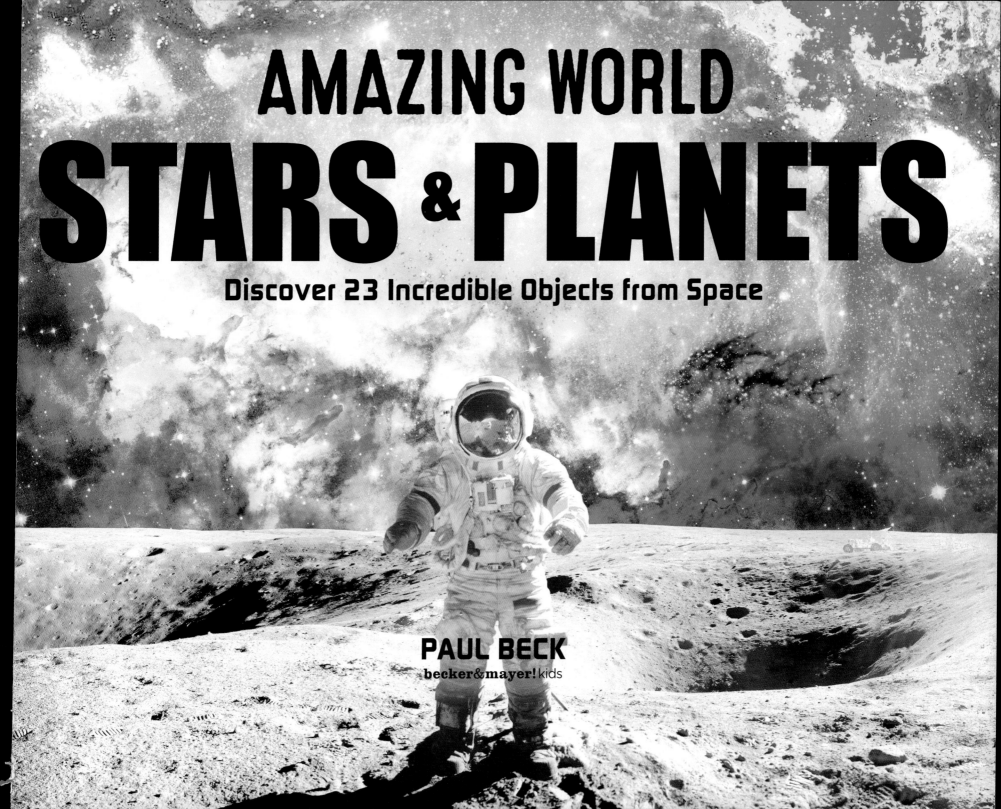

# AMAZING WORLD
# STARS & PLANETS

## Discover 23 Incredible Objects from Space

**PAUL BECK**

becker&mayer! kids

Brimming with creative inspiration, how-to projects, and useful
information to enrich your everyday life, Quarto Knows is a favorite
destination for those pursuing their interests and passions. Visit our
site and dig deeper with our books into your area of interest:
Quarto Creates, Quarto Cooks, Quarto Homes, Quarto Lives,
Quarto Drives, Quarto Explores, Quarto Gifts, or Quarto Kids.

© 2017 Quarto Publishing Group USA Inc.

First Published in 2017 by becker&mayer! kids, an imprint of The Quarto Group.
11120 NE 33rd Place, Suite 101, Bellevue, WA 98004, USA.
T (425) 827-7120  F (425) 828-9659  **www.QuartoKnows.com**

becker&mayer! kids titles are also available at discount for retail, wholesale, promotional, and bulk purchase. For details, contact the Special Sales Manager by email at specialsales@quarto.com or by mail at The Quarto Group, Attn: Special Sales Manager, 401 Second Avenue North, Suite 310, Minneapolis, MN 55401 USA.

17 18 19 20 21 5 4 3 2 1

ISBN: 978-0-7603-5537-4

Library of Congress Cataloging-in-Publication Data is available.

Author: Paul Beck
Design: Megan Haggerty
Editorial: Ashley McPhee
Production: Olivia Holmes
Image research: Farley Bookout
Product development: Blake Mitchum

Printed, manufactured, and assembled in Shenzhen, China, 07/17.

Image credits: All photographs and design elements provided by:
©Shutterstock.com
NASA (National Aeronautics and Space Administration): http://www.nasa.gov
Hubble Space Telescope: http://hubblesite.org
ESA (European Space Agency): http://www.esa.int/ESA

171013

# CONTENTS

# STARS AND PLANETS

It's easy to see stars and planets. All you have to do is go outside! At night, away from city lights, the sky is filled with stars. Some are just like the sun. Others are smaller, and still others are much, much bigger. They're all so amazingly far away that we see them only as tiny points of light. There are planets, too—six that you can see from Earth without a telescope. Each is an amazing world of its own. They're much, much closer than the stars but still just points of light in the nighttime sky.

## SPACE TRAVEL

Believe it or not, you're zipping through space at an amazing speed right now. The earth is spinning fast enough to make one turn every day. Our whole planet is speeding around the sun at more than 67,000 mph (108,000 km/h). The solar system—that's the sun and everything that orbits around it, including planets, dwarf planets, moons, asteroids, and comets—is zipping around the disc of the Milky Way galaxy at almost 450,000 mph (720,000 km/h).

The sun is just one of billions of stars in the galaxy, and our galaxy is just one of billions in the universe. Space is an amazingly big place!

Imagine a dime. Now imagine someone holding up that dime a quarter of a block away. That's how big the piece of sky shown in this picture is. Each of the swirls, circles, and dots in the image is a whole galaxy. There are about 5,500 of them in the picture.

# AMAZING WORLD . . . AND BEYOND

Human explorers have traveled as far as the moon. Our robotic space probes have gone even farther, all the way out of our solar system and into the space beyond. But that's only a tiny, tiny (tiny!) piece of the amazing universe. With the help of telescopes, we can see much farther. In this book, you'll get to see what the telescopes see: planets, stars, giant clouds of glowing gas, galaxies, and more!

Are you ready for a trip that's out of this world? Just turn the page.

# THE SUN

The sun is a star at the center of our solar system. Earth and the other planets orbit around it. Like all stars, it's a glowing ball of super-hot gas. The heart of the sun is a nuclear-powered furnace. There, the nuclear reaction called fusion squashes hydrogen atoms together to form helium, releasing huge amounts of energy. The temperature inside the sun is about 27,000,000°F (15,000,000°C). The sun is a medium-sized star, but compared to Earth, it's huge! It's more than 100 times as wide as our whole planet.

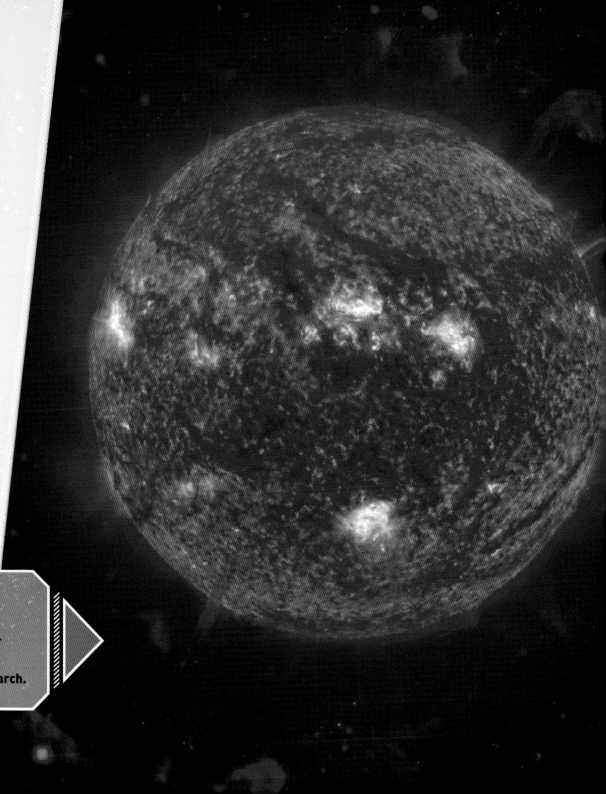

This image shows the sun's atmosphere. You can see a huge arch of glowing gas called a solar prominence (PRAH-muh-nunce). Many Earths would fit under the arch.

← **Solar Prominence**

# VISIBLE SUN

The sun is made of gas. The outer layer, the one that we can see from Earth, is called the photosphere. In this picture, you can also see sunspots. Sunspots are cooler areas in the photosphere. The average sunspot is as wide as the whole planet Earth. The perfect, dark circle in the upper left isn't a sunspot. It's the planet Venus, crossing in front of our view of the sun. This picture is a composite, one image made up of many pictures taken during the six hours it took for Venus to travel from one side of the sun to the other.

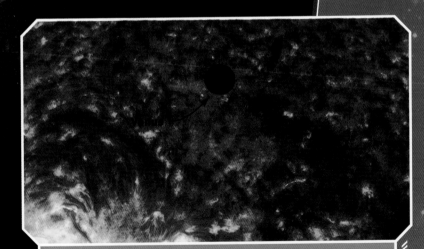

**The last time Venus crossed between the earth and the sun was in 2004. This picture shows the path Venus took past the sun. This is the rarest predictable solar event: It won't happen again until 2117.**

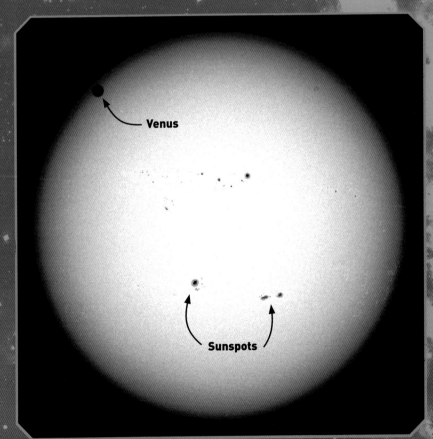

Venus

Sunspots

# MERCURY

Mercury is the closest planet to the sun. It is the most dense planet in our solar system, second only to Earth. It's also the smallest true planet in our solar system. Mercury is only a little bigger than Earth's moon. It kind of looks like a moon, too! The planet, which is made of mostly iron, is covered with craters from meteoroids and comets hitting the surface.

One day on Mercury is as long as two months on Earth!

It's broiling hot on the sunny side of the planet. On the dark side, it gets colder than the deepest deep-freeze.

## WATER

There is water on Mercury! It's in the form of ice, at the bottom of deep craters near the north and south poles. The sun's light and heat never reach there. The ice is left over from comets that crashed into the planet.

# VENUS

Venus is the second planet from the sun. Some people call it our sister planet because it's almost the same size as Earth. But it's not a place where humans (or anything else!) could live. You cannot breathe on Venus because the air is mostly made of carbon dioxide. The planet's atmosphere traps the sun's heat like a greenhouse. The temperature on the surface of the planet is more than 860°F (460°C)! It is the hottest planet in the solar system.

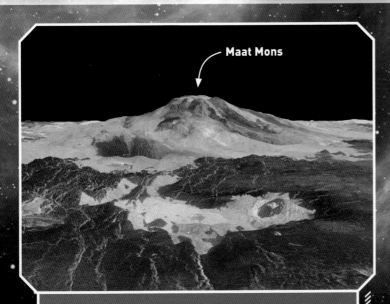

Maat Mons

**Maat Mons is a volcano near Venus's equator.**

The clouds on Venus are made of sulfuric acid!

## ALWAYS CLOUDY

Thick clouds cover the whole planet, so it's impossible to see Venus's surface from Earth or space.

# EARTH

Our planet is third from the sun. It is the fifth-largest planet in our solar system. From space, it looks like a big, blue ball with swirling white clouds. It's the only planet in our solar system where there's always liquid water on the surface. Water covers more than two thirds of our planet.

Moon ⟶

## JUST RIGHT FOR LIFE

So far, Earth is the only place known to have life of any kind. It orbits the sun in the "Goldilocks zone," where it's not too hot, not too cold, but just right for liquid water to exist. There can be no life without water.

⟵ Earth

The crew of the *Apollo 17* spacecraft took this picture of Earth on their way to the moon in 1972. You can see Antarctica at the bottom of the photo, with Africa above it.

← Sun

# MARS

Nicknamed the "Red Planet," Mars gets its color from iron in the rocks and soil. Mars is about half the size of Earth and is the fourth planet from the sun. Like Venus, its air is mostly carbon dioxide. There's water on Mars, but it's all frozen under the surface and in the polar ice caps. Temperatures on Mars can plunge as low as -225°F (-143°C).

**This full-planet picture of Mars shows craters, volcanoes, and a deep chain of canyons called the Valles Marineris that's as long as the United States is wide!**

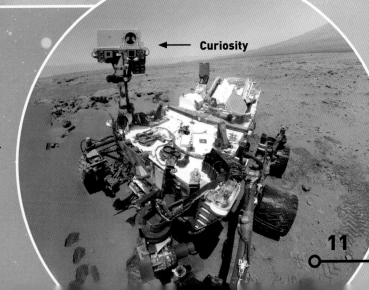
← Curiosity

## ROVER SELFIE

The Curiosity Mars rover took this selfie on the planet's surface. Astronomers put many images together to create a photo that leaves out the rover's robot arm. Curiosity is the size of a car and weighs 1 ton (907 kg). Human explorers hope to travel to the Red Planet in the future.

More spacecraft have visited Mars than any other planet besides Earth. So far, 23 robotic probes have orbited, landed, or roved across its surface.

Jupiter is 11 times as big across as Earth!

# JUPITER

Our solar system's biggest planet isn't made of rock. It's a giant ball of gas called a gas giant. It's made mostly of hydrogen and helium. There's no solid surface on the planet. Far down in the atmosphere, gigantic pressure creates an ocean of liquid hydrogen. Jupiter may have as many as 67 moons. So far, there are 53 confirmed ones.

## STORMY STRIPES AND SWIRLS

Jupiter is covered with clouds in a pattern of stripes and swirls. The white bands, called zones, are high clouds of ammonia ice crystals. The colored bands, called belts, are lower in the atmosphere. The swirls are huge, rotating storms.

The Great Red Spot is a permanent storm south of Jupiter's equator. It's twice as wide as the whole Earth!

The Great Red Spot

The small sphere to the left is Jupiter's third-largest moon, Io. It may look tiny in the picture, but Io is actually about the size of Earth's moon. It's about as far from the tops of the planet's clouds as our own moon is from Earth. There are more than 100 active volcanoes spewing lava onto Io's rocky surface. Some shoot out plumes of gas and dust hundreds of miles high. When space rocks hit the surface and form craters, lava flows out to fill them with lakes of liquid rock.

# SATURN

Sixth from the sun, Saturn is the second-biggest planet in the solar system. Like Jupiter, it's a gas giant made mostly of hydrogen and helium. Its yellow-tan color comes from crystals of frozen ammonia in the upper clouds. Saturn has 53 confirmed moons, with as many as 9 more possible moons.

Saturn is the farthest planet you can see from Earth without a telescope. It looks like a bright, yellowish star.

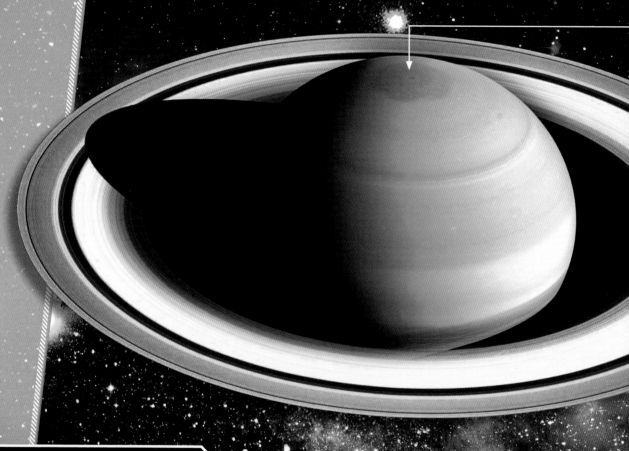

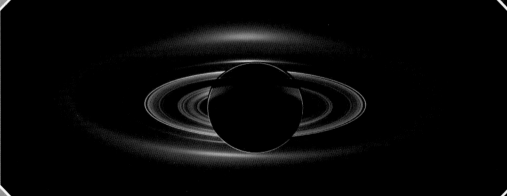

This picture combines 141 images from the Cassini spacecraft. It shows Saturn from the far side, with the sun blocked behind the planet.

A 220-mph (360 km/h) wind current called a jet stream creates the six-sided shape at the top of Saturn. There's a swirling storm at the center.

# RINGS

Saturn is known for its beautiful rings. There are more than 1,000 of them. The rings are made mostly of particles of water ice. (You'd probably just call it "ice," but astronomers say "water ice" because of the many other types of frozen material in the solar system.)

There are dark gaps between Saturn's rings. These are areas where the ice particles have been cleared away by the pull of gravity from the planet's moons. The biggest gap is called the Cassini Division, named after the Italian astronomer who discovered it through his telescope more than 300 years ago. (The Cassini spacecraft also has his name.) Saturn's moon Mimas keeps the Cassini Division clear of ice particles.

Saturn casts a shadow on its own rings in this picture from the Cassini space probe.

# URANUS

Uranus is the sixth planet from the sun and the third-largest in the solar system. It was the first planet discovered with the help of a telescope. The English astronomer William Herschel found it in 1871. Uranus is an ice giant, with a thick, slushy ocean around a solid core. The slush is made of water, ammonia, and methane. Methane is the main ingredient in the natural gas that powers stoves and furnaces on Earth. Uranus also has 13 rings and 27 moons.

The Voyager 2 spacecraft sent this picture as it flew by Uranus in 1986.

## TIPPED OVER AND BACKWARD

Uranus is tipped over on its side. It spins on an axis that's almost horizontal compared to all the other planets. Like Venus, it also spins from east to west. The planet's strange tilt may have been caused by another planet-sized object running into it when Uranus was young.

This picture is a false-color image. The colors were added to show cloud features detected by the Hubble Space Telescope but invisible to human eyes. The blue color shows where the atmosphere is clearer. The yellow and gray are areas with thicker clouds.

This "ice" is actually superhot! Gigantic pressure from gravity heats it to 9,000°F (5,000°C), at the same time squashing it to slush.

# NEPTUNE

More than 170 years ago, a French mathematician named Urbain Le Verrier predicted the location of Neptune before it was ever found. Astronomers noticed that the planet Uranus didn't orbit the sun the way they expected it to. Le Verrier thought the cause was another planet. He used math to predict where it would be. Sure enough, it was found there right away.

Neptune is the most distant true planet in our solar system. It's so far out that it takes 165 Earth years to travel once around the sun. That means only one Neptunian year has passed since the planet was discovered in 1846. Like Uranus, Neptune is an ice giant. It's the four-largest planet in the solar system.

When Voyager 2 passed by Neptune in 1989, the spacecraft's cameras sent back pictures showing the fast-moving oval in the middle of this picture, called the Great Dark Spot. When astronomers aimed the Hubble Space Telescope at the planet five years later, the spot was gone!

Triton →

**Neptune has 13 known moons. This picture shows the curve of the planet and its largest moon, Triton.**

# SUPERSONIC WINDS

Neptune has the fastest winds in the solar system. The strongest ones clock in at nearly 750 mph (1,200 km/h), faster than the speed of sound on Earth. When Voyager 2 passed by Neptune in 1989, it spotted a speedy white cloud nicknamed "Scooter." It's the triangle-shaped cloud in this picture. Scooter zipped around the whole planet in just 16 hours.

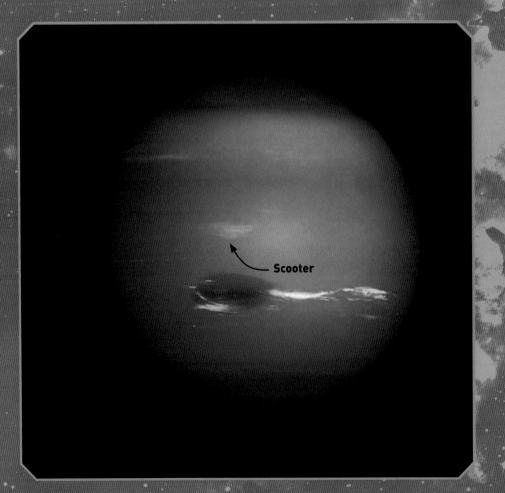

Scooter

# PLUTO

Pluto was named by Venetia Burney, an 11-year-old English girl.

In 1930, an astronomer named Clyde Tombaugh discovered a brand-new planet called Pluto. But Pluto was a bit weird compared to the other planets. It was tiny, even smaller than Earth's moon. It's path crossed Neptune's, bringing Pluto closer to the sun for part of its orbit. For more than 70 years, Pluto was known as the ninth planet. But then astronomers discovered two new planet-like objects beyond Pluto, named Eris and Makemake (mah-kee-mah-kee). Scientists began thinking about what exactly it takes to be a planet. They decided that Eris and Makemake—and Pluto!—were something else: dwarf planets.

## WHAT'S THE DIFFERENCE?

Dwarf planets are a lot like true planets, only smaller. Both orbit the sun. Both are big enough for their own gravity to pull them into ball shapes. (That makes them different from comets and asteroids, which have all kinds of shapes.) But true planets have clear paths around the sun. Dwarf planets' orbits are cluttered up with space rocks. The dwarf planets' gravity isn't strong enough to clear them out of the way.

Pluto has three moons. The largest, Charon, is almost half as big as Pluto itself. Charon is big and round enough to count as a dwarf planet on its own, so some astronomers call the two of them together a double dwarf planet system.

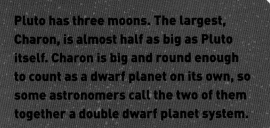

Charon ←

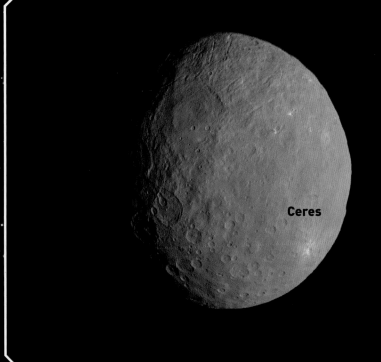

Ceres

← Pluto

Pluto, Eris, and Makemake all orbit far from the sun, in a zone called the Kuiper (KYE-per) Belt. But there's one dwarf planet closer to Earth. It's tiny Ceres (SIH-reez), in the Asteroid Belt between Mars and Jupiter.

# THE MOON

Most of the planets in our solar system have moons. In fact, most have more than one. Earth is the only planet with just one moon. Our moon is the fifth-largest in the solar system. It's about a quarter of the size of our planet, and it helps keep the earth's orbit steady around the sun.

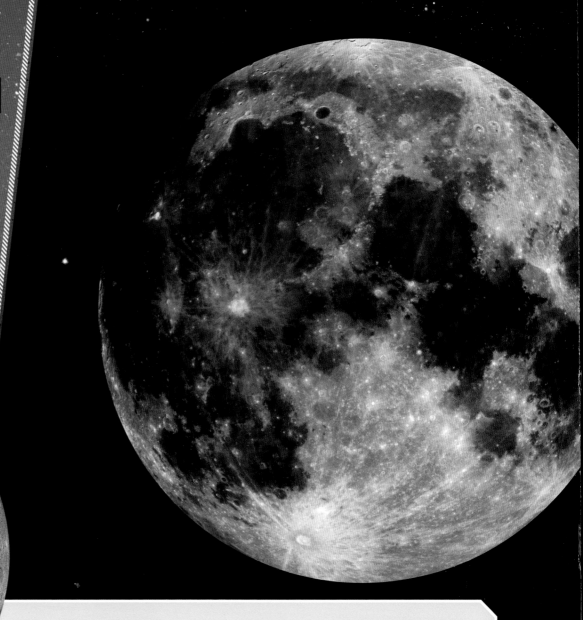

Unlike other planets' moons, Earth's moon doesn't really have a name. Most people just call it "the moon." As the moon travels around the earth, it turns so that the same side is always facing the planet. That means we never get to see the other side from Earth. This picture of the moon's far side was put together from images taken by the Lunar Reconnaissance Orbiter spacecraft.

The moon is covered with craters left when comets, meteoroids, and asteroids smashed into the surface. You can see the big, dark areas from Earth when you look at the full moon. They're called maria (MAH-ree-uh). If there's just one, it's mare (MAH-ray). That's Latin for "sea," but the maria aren't seas at all. They're crater basins that filled with molten lava when the moon was young.

# BORN FROM EARTH

Scientists think the moon formed when a huge space rock (about the size of Mars!) smashed into the young earth. The crash blew bits of Earth and the space rock into orbit. Over time, gravity pulled the smashed-up bits together to form the moon.

The moon is the only place outside Earth that has been visited by humans. Only twelve people have ever walked on its surface.

# EUROPA

Europa is Jupiter's fourth-largest moon. It's just a little smaller than Earth's moon. Its surface is covered with water ice. Scientists think there's a very deep ocean of liquid water under the ice.

Europa was one of the first moons ever discovered around a planet beyond Earth. The Italian astronomer Galileo spotted Jupiter's four largest moons with his telescope more than 400 years ago. For that reason, they're called the Galilean Moons.

Europa is one of the most likely places in the solar system to have life.

## GEYSER PLUMES

Astronomers using the Hubble Space Telescope have spotted 100-mile-high plumes of vapor shooting up from Europa's surface. The vapor may be water, more evidence for an ocean under the ice.

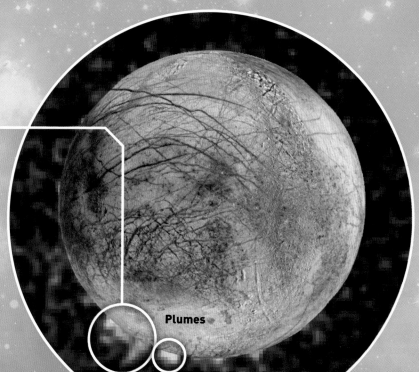

Plumes

Europa's orbit is slightly elliptical, or oval-shaped. That means its distance from Jupiter changes slightly as it travels around the planet. The changes in distance cause slight differences in the pull of Jupiter's gravity on Europa. The gravity changes result in tides that stretch and relax the surface of the moon, creating crisscrossing cracks in the ice like in this picture. The color in the picture was adjusted to help show the details.

# TITAN

Titan is bigger than the planet Mercury! It's Saturn's largest moon. Titan is also the second-biggest moon in the solar system, just a bit smaller than Jupiter's largest moon, Ganymede. It's the only moon in our solar system with a thick atmosphere and clouds.

The surface temperature of Titan is -290°F (-179°C), so cold that there are rivers and lakes of liquid ethane and methane. (Methane is the main ingredient in natural gas on Earth.) These liquids sometimes even fall from the sky as rain. There's water on Titan, too, but of course it's all solid ice.

This picture of Titan was put together from images taken by the Cassini spacecraft. It shows the moon in infrared (IR) light, invisible to humans without special cameras. The infrared view shows the surface beneath Titan's thick clouds.

# SOLAR SYSTEM MOON COUNT

Here's what Titan looks like in visible light. It's a fuzzy disk completely covered with thick, yellow clouds.

Titan is the only place in the outer part of our solar system where a spacecraft has landed. The Huygens (HOY-guns) space probe parachuted to its surface in 2005.

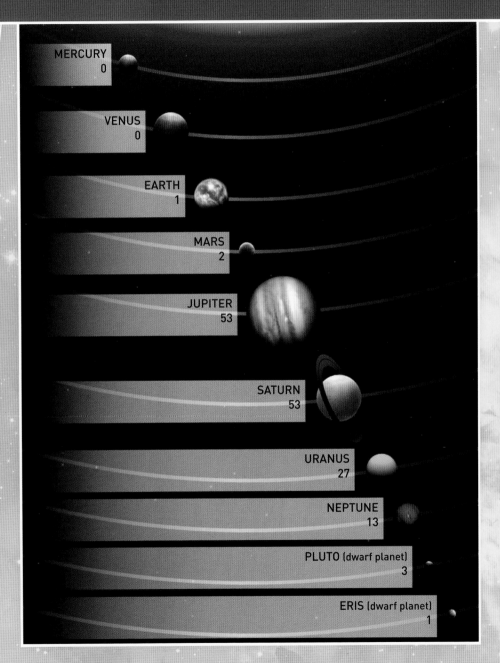

MERCURY
0

VENUS
0

EARTH
1

MARS
2

JUPITER
53

SATURN
53

URANUS
27

NEPTUNE
13

PLUTO (dwarf planet)
3

ERIS (dwarf planet)
1

# COMETS

Some people call comets "dirty snowballs." But they're snowballs the size of whole cities! And they're not really made of snow. Comets are mostly ice—frozen water and carbon dioxide ($CO_2$), along with other gases. Mixed in with the ice, there's dust, rock, and some organic material. Organic means the material contains carbon.

Like planets, dwarf planets, and asteroids, comets travel around the sun. For most of their journey, they're far from the sun, out in the Kuiper Belt with Pluto and the other dwarf planets. Some come from even farther away.

## COMA AND TAIL

When a comet's orbit brings it close to the sun, the ice starts to warm up. It goes straight from solid to gas without melting into a liquid in between. (That's called sublimation—SUB-lih-MAY-shun.) A fuzzy halo of gas and dust, called the coma, begins to surround the comet. Along with light and heat, the sun puts out a stream of particles called the solar wind. As the comet gets even closer, this particle stream pushes gas and dust from the coma out into a long tail.

The tail always points away from the sun. A comet's tail can stretch as far as a million miles!

This picture from the European Space Agency's Rosetta spacecraft shows the comet named 67P/Churyumov-Gerasimenko. Jets of gas and dust are shooting up from its surface as it begins to warm up.

Comets really have two tails. One is made of dust and the other is made of gas. The dust tail reflects sunlight. It usually looks white or yellow. The gas tail glows with its own light as waves of invisible ultraviolet (UV) light pass through it. The gas tail is often blue.

# ORION NEBULA

The Orion Nebula (NEB-you-luh) is a stellar nursery, or a place in space where stars are born. It's part of the constellation Orion. A nebula is a giant cloud of gas and dust. Some nebulae (NEB-you-lee, the word for more than one) are dark. They block our view of the stars behind them. Others reflect the light of nearby stars. Still others, like the Orion Nebula, glow with light of their own. The glow happens when invisible waves of ultraviolet (UV) light pass through the clouds of gas. The UV light waves come from large, young stars inside the nebula.

The amazing shapes and colors of nebulae can only be seen in photos taken by powerful telescopes. This picture of the Orion Nebula is a combination of hundreds of different photos from the Hubble Space Telescope.

# A STAR IS BORN

A star begins to form when gravity pulls clouds of gas and dust into a huge, spinning ball called a protostar. Gravity keeps pulling the protostar into a smaller and smaller ball. As the atoms of gas get squashed closer and closer together, the ball gets hotter and hotter. If the temperature rises above 24,000,000°F (13,000,000°C), nuclear fusion starts, and a star is born!

Depending on its size, it can take many millions of years for a protostar to become a star.

**You can see the Orion Nebula in the winter and spring sky using just your eyes. It looks like a bright star in the middle of Orion's sword below the three stars of his belt.**

# EAGLE NEBULA

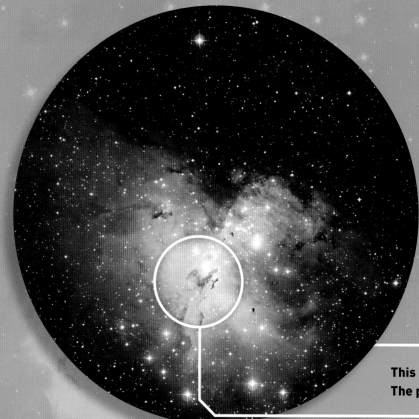

These huge clouds of gas and dust in the image to the right are nicknamed the "Pillars of Creation." They're part of a bigger, glowing cloud called the Eagle Nebula. At the tip of the tallest pillar, you can see fingers of gas with blob-like tips stitching out into space. Each blob is bigger than our whole solar system! They're the beginnings of new stars.

**This is a picture of the whole Eagle Nebula. The pillars are in the middle of the image.**

## STAR COLORS

If you look at the stars on a clear night away from city lights, you'll notice that different stars have different colors. The color depends on the temperature of the star's photosphere, or "surface." Red stars are the coolest. (Cool for a star—they're still really, really hot!) Yellow stars like the sun are medium-hot. Blue stars are the hottest.

| 5,000°F (2,760°C) | 10,000°F (5,538°C) | 7,000°F (3,871°C) |
|---|---|---|

| 12,000°F (6,649°C) | 15,000°F (8,316°C) | 35,000°F (19,427°C) | 60,000°F (33,316°C) |
|---|---|---|---|

Ultraviolet light from these stars makes the nebula gases glow.

# BUBBLE NEBULA

The Bubble Nebula is so big that light takes more than 7 years to travel from one side to the other. The bubble is being "blown" by the bright star just above and to the left of the center of the nebula. It's a huge, superhot blue star more than 45 times the size of our sun. The star shoots gas from its atmosphere out into space. The gas travels as fast as 4,000,000 mph (6,440,000 km/h)!

The star is surrounded by a cloud of cool gas. As the stellar wind blows out from the star in all directions, it pushes the gas cloud molecules together like the pile of snow in front of a snowplow. This shell of compressed (pushed-together) gas is the "skin" of the bubble.

The Bubble Nebula is so far away that light from its star takes 7,100 years to reach our solar system. So when we look at the glowing bubble, we're seeing it the way it was more than 2,500 years before the Great Pyramid was built.

# HUBBLE SPACE TELESCOPE

The picture of the Bubble Nebula is a combination of four images from the Hubble Space Telescope. The telescope has been in Earth orbit since 1990. Because orbiting telescopes like Hubble are above Earth's atmosphere, they have a clearer view of space than ground-based telescopes do.

Space is so big that astronomers measure it in light-years. One light-year is the distance light travels in a year. That's 6 trillion (6,000,000,000,000) miles! Light is the fastest thing there is.

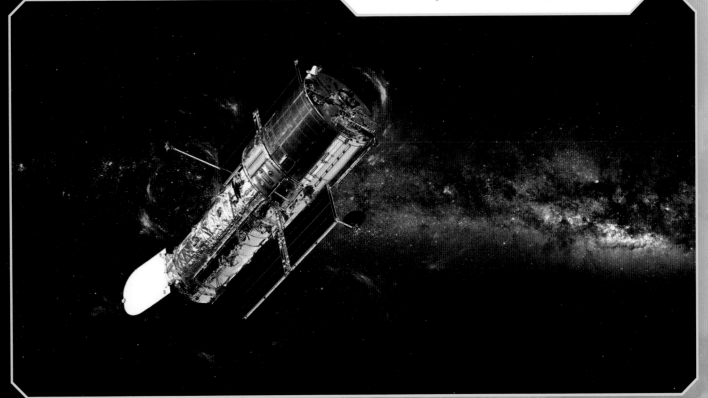

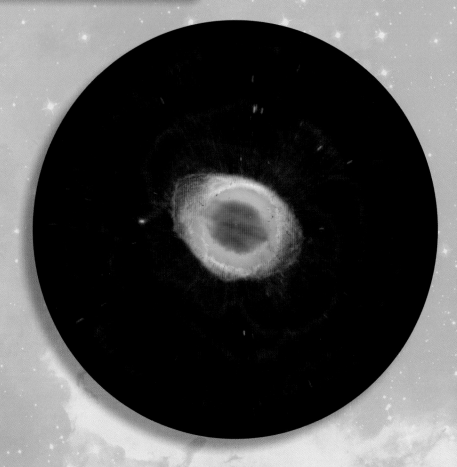

# RING NEBULA

The Ring Nebula is a type of gas cloud called a planetary nebula. When a star gets close to the end of its life, nuclear fusion stars burning in a shell around the core. The star swells to giant size, and the outside cools to red. The star has become a red giant. A sun-sized star can keep burning as a red giant for a billion years or more. After that, the outer layers get pushed off into space to become a planetary nebula. The leftover core stops burning and shrinks. It becomes a small, hot ball of gas called a white dwarf.

## A STAR'S LIFE

The smaller the star, the longer it burns. Our sun was born more than 4.5 billion years ago. It will burn for another 5 billion years before becoming a red giant. Smaller stars burn even longer. But really gigantic stars put out much more energy. They can burn up all their fuel in just a few million years.

The Ring Nebula is about 1 light-year across. It's a little more than 2,000 light-years from our solar system.

A planetary nebula doesn't have anything to do with planets. The name comes from the British astronomer William Hershel. He lived a long time ago, from 1783 to 1822. Herschel studied the Ring Nebula through his telescope. He thought it looked like a planet, so he called it a planetary nebula. The name stuck.

# CAT'S EYE NEBULA

The Cat's Eye Nebula is another planetary nebula. It's made of gas thrown off by a dying star. What's left of the star will shrink to become a white dwarf. The star that created this nebula put out material in several bursts. The bursts were about 1,500 years apart. Each burst traveled away from the star in a growing, bubble-like shell. The expanding shells created the bull's-eye pattern in the picture. It's a little like the layers of a sliced onion.

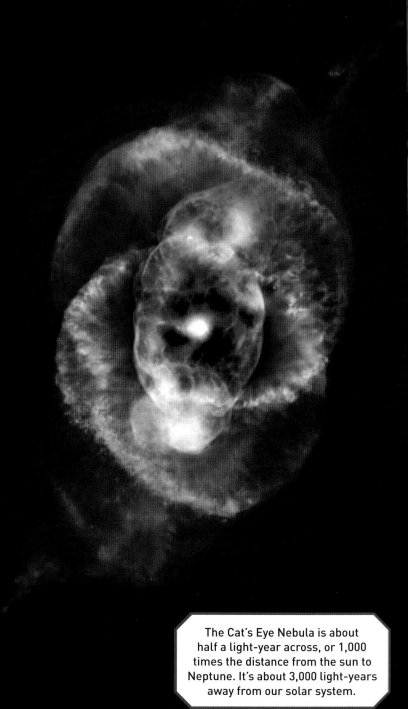

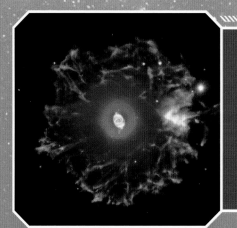

This image from the Earth-based Nordic Optical Telescope shows a huge, very faint cloud of gas around the bright Cat's Eye Nebula in the center.

The Cat's Eye Nebula is about half a light-year across, or 1,000 times the distance from the sun to Neptune. It's about 3,000 light-years away from our solar system.

This picture is a combination of images from the Hubble Space Telescope and the Chandra X-Ray Observatory. The red, orange, and purple parts show the light we can see. The blue part in the center shows what we would see if we could see X-rays.

# DIFFERENT TELESCOPES FOR DIFFERENT WAVES

Light, X-rays, and even radio waves are all the same form of energy, called electromagnetic energy. Electromagnetic energy travels in waves. The light we can see is just a small part of the range of all electromagnetic waves, called the electromagnetic spectrum. All electromagnetic waves travel at the same speed. It's the speed of light, 186,000 miles per second (300,000 km/s). That's the fastest speed there is. Nothing can travel faster.

The difference between the different parts of the spectrum is the wavelength. That's the distance between the wave peaks. Stars and other space objects put out many different kinds of electromagnetic energy. Most of it is invisible to human eyes. To learn as much as possible about the universe, astronomers use different types of telescopes to see different kinds of waves.

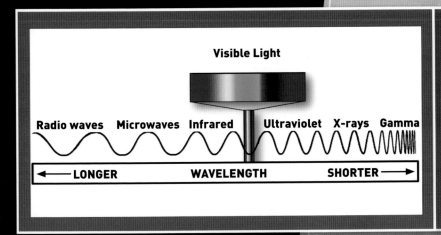

Visible Light

Radio waves   Microwaves   Infrared   Ultraviolet   X-rays   Gamma

← LONGER        WAVELENGTH        SHORTER →

| TELESCOPE | WHAT IT DETECTS |
| --- | --- |
| Arecibo Telescope | Radio waves |
| Spitzer Space Telescope | Infrared waves |
| Hubble Space Telescope | Visible light waves (also ultraviolet and infrared) |
| Chandra X-Ray Observatory | X-rays |
| Swift Orbiting Observatory | Gamma rays |

# CRAB NEBULA

About 1,000 years ago, astronomers in China wrote about a brand-new star that had appeared in the sky. It grew so bright that it could be seen during the day. Then it faded away. What they had seen was a large star exploding at the end of its life. If you look through a telescope, you can see what's left of that star. It's called the Crab Nebula. An explosion like the one that created the Crab Nebula is called a supernova.

## BIG STAR, BIG EXPLOSION

If a star has more than eight times the mass (amount of material) of the sun, it doesn't create a planetary nebula and white dwarf at the end of its life. Instead, it explodes in a supernova. Most of the star gets blown into space. What's left collapses under its own gravity.

If the supernova's star had less than 25 times the mass of the sun, the leftover part collapses into a fast-spinning ball called a neutron star. A neutron star contains as much material as the sun, squashed into a ball the size of a city. If the supernova's star had more than 25 times the mass of the sun, the leftover part collapses into an even smaller ball. The ball has so much material in such a small space that even light can't escape its gravity. It's called a black hole.

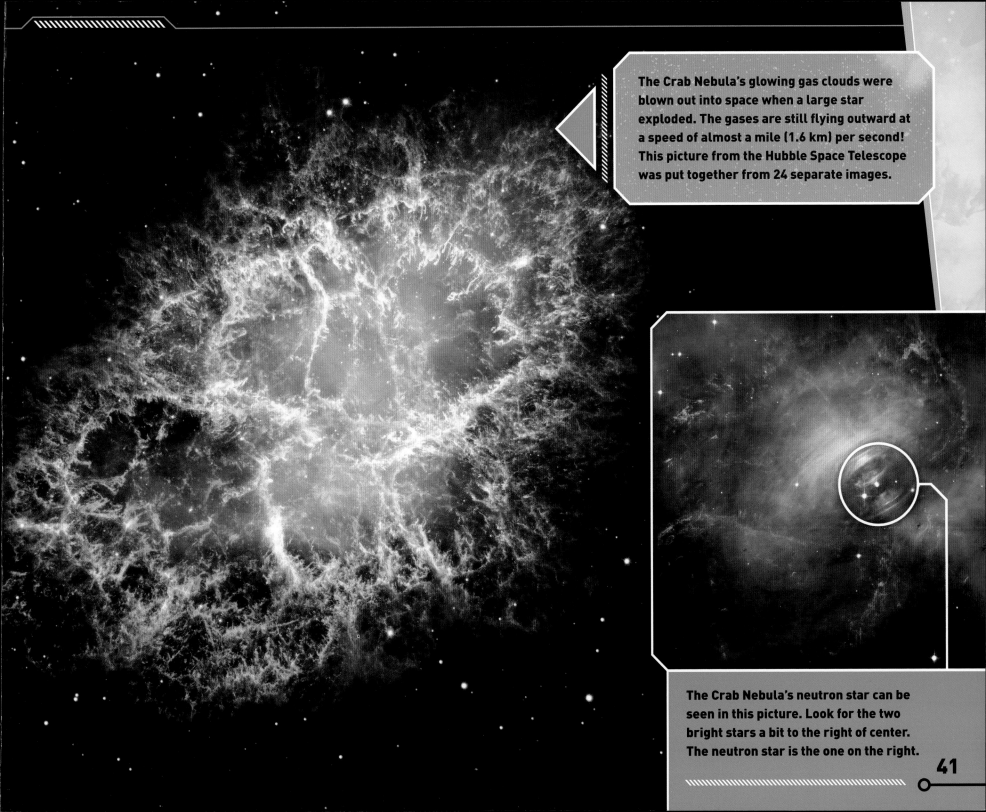

The Crab Nebula's glowing gas clouds were blown out into space when a large star exploded. The gases are still flying outward at a speed of almost a mile (1.6 km) per second! This picture from the Hubble Space Telescope was put together from 24 separate images.

The Crab Nebula's neutron star can be seen in this picture. Look for the two bright stars a bit to the right of center. The neutron star is the one on the right.

# ANDROMEDA GALAXY

A galaxy is a huge collection of stars, solar systems, gas, and dust, all held together by gravity. Galaxies are so gigantic that it's hard to imagine their size. They can be hundreds of thousands or even millions of light-years across. (Remember, a light-year is 6,000,000,000,000 miles!) They hold billions and billions of stars.

The Andromeda Galaxy is the closest spiral galaxy to our own, the Milky Way. It's shaped like our galaxy, too: a spinning, many-armed spiral with a thick bulge in the middle. It measures about 220,000 light-years from side to side. That's twice the size of the Milky Way.

This Hubble Space Telescope image shows about one third of the Andromeda Galaxy. It's the biggest, sharpest picture ever taken of our neighbor.

On a dark night away from city lights, you can see the Andromeda Galaxy without a telescope. It looks like a faint smudge in the sky. At 2.5 million light-years away, it's the biggest, farthest thing you can see with your eyes alone.

## CRASH COMING!

The Andromeda Galaxy and Milky Way are headed straight for each other at more than 400,000 mph! In about four billion years, they'll smash together. Don't worry, the stars themselves are spaced so far apart that they'll miss one another. But eventually the two galaxies will be joined together into one super-sized galaxy.

## GALAXY SHAPES

Galaxies come in different shapes. About two-thirds of them are big spirals like Andromeda and our own Milky Way. Others, the largest galaxies, are shaped like fat footballs. Still others are smaller, irregular shapes. Andromeda is the nearest spiral galaxy, but there are other, smaller irregular galaxies that are closer to the Milky Way.

**This picture of a different galaxy, called the Pinwheel, gives a good view of its spiral arms.**

# THE MILKY WAY

On dark nights away from bright lights, our own galaxy shows as a milky band stretching across the whole sky. We can't see its spiral disc shape because we're inside it. Instead, we see the disc edge-on. Our galaxy has a super-massive black hole at the center. It is hidden from us by dark clouds of gas and dust.

Our galaxy is about 100,000 light-years from side to side. (That's 600,000,000,000,000,000,000 miles!) It contains about 200 billion stars. We're in the spiral arm called the Sagittarius Arm, in a small branch called the Orion Spur.

## THREE GALAXIES

This picture from Chile shows the Milky Way along with our two closest neighbor galaxies, called the Magellanic Clouds. Look for the two fuzzy patches to the right. They're dwarf galaxies, much closer than the Andromeda Galaxy but not spiral-shaped.

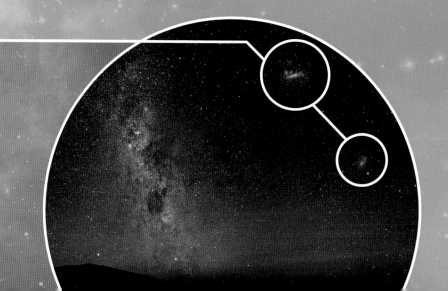

45

# SOMBRERO GALAXY

The Sombrero Galaxy is half the width of the Milky Way, but it has four times as many stars. From Earth, we see a dark rim of dust clouds that looks a bit like the wide brim of a hat. The dust rings in the galaxy's disc contain lots of young, bright stars. Like the Milky Way, the Sombrero Galaxy probably has a super-massive black hole in the bulge at its center. The Sombrero Galaxy measures 50,000 light-years from edge to edge. It contains more than 700 billion stars. The galaxy is about 30 million light-years from Earth. The light that created this picture left the galaxy tens of millions of years before there were humans on Earth.

This picture of a different galaxy, called NGC 7049, shows dark lanes of dust against the glow of millions of stars.

Astronomers think almost all galaxies have black holes at their centers.

# BIG NUMBERS

Numbers and distances in space are gigantic. If you learn about a million miles or a billion stars, what does that really mean? Here's one way to think about it: If you count one number every second, it takes 100 seconds to count to 100—a little over a minute and a half. If you wanted to count to just one million, and if you could to it without eating, sleeping, or doing anything else, you'd be counting for 11-1/2 days. If you wanted to count to a billion, it would take you nearly 32 years! (You've got better things to do with your time.)

This picture from the Spitzer Space Telescope shows the Sombrero Galaxy in infrared light. The infrared image shows that the ring of dust around the outside is much wider than it looks in the visible light picture.

# GLOSSARY

**Asteroid**
An orbiting space rock. A large number of asteroids orbit the sun in the zone called the Asteroid Belt, between Mars and Jupiter.

**Black hole**
A space object with so much matter squashed into such a small space that even light can't escape its gravity.

**Carbon dioxide**
A compound consisting of one atom of carbon and two atoms of oxygen.

**Comet**
An orbiting, city-sized chunk of ice and dust. When a comet's orbit takes it close to the sun, gases and dust form a long tail.

**Constellation**
A group of stars seen from Earth as an imaginary picture, like a dot-to-dot picture.

**Dwarf planet**
A large object orbiting a star, big enough for its own gravity to form it into a ball but too small to clear other space rocks out of its orbit.

**Equator**
An imaginary line around a planet, star, or moon, halfway between the poles.

**Galaxy**
A huge system of gas, dust, and billions of stars held together by gravity.

**Gas giant**
A huge planet made of gas.

**Gravity**
A force that attracts all objects to one another. The larger and closer the object, the stronger the force.

**Helium**
An element with atoms consisting of two protons, two neutrons, and two electrons.

**Hydrogen**
The most common element in the universe. Its atoms have one proton and one electron.

**Ice giant**
A huge planet made of hot, slushy "ice."

**Infrared light**
Light energy with a wavelength longer than visible light. Infrared means "lower than red," due to its place in the electromagnetic spectrum.

**Meteoroid**
A small space rock. If a meteoroid enters Earth's atmosphere and makes it all the way to the surface without burning up, it's a meteorite.

**Moon**
A natural satellite orbiting around a planet.

**Nebula**
A huge cloud of gas and dust in space.

**Nuclear fusion**
An atomic reaction that fuses atoms together to create new atoms, releasing large amounts of energy in the process.

**Orbit**
The curved path of an astronomical object around a star, planet, or moon.

**Photosphere**
The visible part of a star; its "surface."

**Planet**
A large object orbiting a star, big enough for its own gravity to form it into a ball and to clear other space rocks out of its orbit.

**Solar system**
A star and everything that orbits around it.

**Star**
A huge ball of burning gas.

**Supernova**
A huge explosion at the end of a very large star's life.

**Terrestrial planet**
A planet made of rock, like Earth.

**Ultraviolet light**
Light energy with a wavelength shorter than visible light. Ultraviolet means "beyond violet," due to its place in the electromagnetic spectrum.

**The universe**
Everything there is!

**White dwarf**
The small, glowing ball of gas left over after a small or medium-sized star sheds its outer layers at the end of its life.